CRAFT TOPICS

# ROMANS AND ANGLO-SAXONS IN BRITAIN

## Nicola Baxter

W
FRANKLIN WATTS
LONDON•SYDNEY

This edition 2008

Franklin Watts
338 Euston Road
London, NW1 3BH

Franklin Watts Australia
Level 17/207 Kent Street
Sydney, NSW 2000

© 1994 Franklin Watts

First published in 1994 as Craft Topics: Invaders
and Settlers

Editor: Hazel Poole
Designer: Sally Boothroyd
Photography: Peter Millard

A CIP catalogue record for this book is available
from the British Library.

ISBN: 978 0 7496 7827 2
Dewey number: 941.01

Printed in Dubai

Franklin Watts is a division of Hachette Children's
Books, an Hachette Livre UK company.

# CONTENTS

# THE FAR EDGE OF EUROPE

From the earliest times, people have travelled from their homes to find better lives for themselves and their families. The new skills, ideas and languages that they bring to the country where they settle may change for ever the lives of the people already living there and the history of the country itself.

*At the time when Celtic peoples were moving westward into Britain, the great civilisations of Greece and Rome grew up around the Mediterranean. From small beginnings in Rome, the Roman Empire spread in all directions. In the first century AD, Britain became the most northerly part of the Roman Empire.*

## A THOUSAND YEARS OF INVASIONS

It is almost a thousand years since Britain was last invaded and conquered by an army from overseas. This was when the Normans, under the leadership of Duke William of Normandy, invaded in 1066. But for a thousand years before that, many different peoples came to settle in the British Isles. They knew that Britain had rich supplies of wood, metal and farmed produce. The changes that these invaders brought to Britain are still part of our lives today.

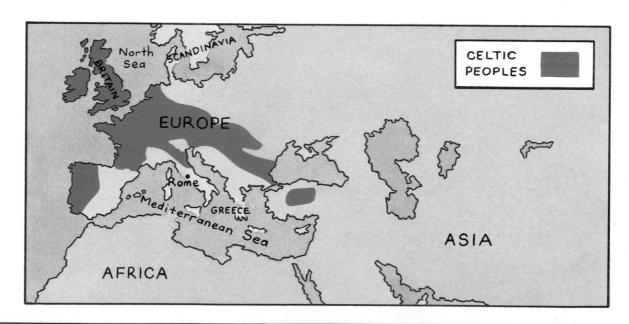

North Sea • SCANDINAVIA • BRITAIN • EUROPE • Rome • Mediterranean Sea • GREECE • AFRICA • ASIA

CELTIC PEOPLES

3500 BC onwards people from western Europe settle in Britain.

55 BC The Roman Julius Caesar arrives in Britain.

AD 43 The Romans invade southern Britain.

AD 406 The Romans leave Britain. The Anglo-Saxons begin to invade northern and eastern Britain.

# THE ANCIENT BRITONS

The people who lived in Britain 2,000 years ago are known as Britons, but they too had come from more eastern parts of Europe. They were of Celtic origin, the ancestors of many of the people who live in Wales today. The roots of their Celtic languages can still be traced in modern Welsh and Gaelic languages.

The time in which the ancient Britons lived is known as the Iron Age because they made and used iron tools. In fact, the Celts were very skilled at working many kinds of metal.

Most Celts lived by farming. Large family groups farmed the land and raised animals for food and clothing. Traces of their fields can sometimes be seen today, but more obvious are the huge mounds of earth that they built to protect themselves from attack.

▲ Many Iron Age earthworks can still be seen. This fort at Maiden Castle in Dorset was protected by four great earth walls.

We cannot read what the Celtic Britons themselves felt and thought because until the Roman invasion they did not read or write. Their knowledge of what had happened came from spoken stories or songs. This is called oral history.

*The Celts in Britain were not isolated from the rest of Europe. Traders brought goods from other parts of the Roman Empire long before the Roman invasion.*

793 The Vikings begin to raid Britain.

878 King Alfred defeats the Vikings.

1066 The Normans invade Britain.

# THE ROMAN INVASION

By the time the Romans invaded Britain in AD 43, they already had a vast empire. They were used to taking over new lands and people and had very efficient armies and army commanders who knew how to take control quickly and completely.

At the time of the invasion, the Romans had already had contact with parts of Britain for nearly a hundred years. In 55 BC Julius Caesar, who had been fighting in what is now France, crossed the Channel and subdued a few tribes. His visit may have been meant only as a warning to the Britons not to help the French tribes fight the Romans.

About 40,000 Roman soldiers took part in the invasion of AD 43. They had better weapons than the British troops and they were more carefully trained and organised. Some tribes fought hard against the invaders, but others were happy to welcome new opportunities to trade with the whole Roman Empire.

As soon as the south-east was secure, the Emperor Claudius himself came to accept the surrender of the local leaders of the British tribes at what is now Colchester in Essex.

*This bronze shield shows the skill of Celtic craftsmen before the Roman invasion. They used beautifully flowing designs to decorate their metalwork. The shield was found in the River Thames.* ▶

▲ *Before they could get close to the Romans, the British soldiers were attacked by a hail of javelins. In close fighting, their longer swords were difficult to use and, unlike the Romans, they had very little armour.*

6

# MAKE A CELTIC SHIELD

*Ask a grown-up to help you with this, as the knife blade will be sharp!*

▲ **1.** Draw a shield shape on the cardboard box, using a plate to shape the corners, and carefully cut it out.

**You will need:** a large piece of thick cardboard ● a small plate ● a modelling knife ● empty plastic food pots and lids of various sizes ● a pencil ● a ruler ● PVA glue ● bronze-coloured paint ● scissors ● coloured paper or plastic "jewels"

**4.** Paint the whole shield a bronze colour and add pieces of coloured paper and plastic "jewels" as decoration.

▲ **2.** Using food pot lids and bases, make a design on your shield. Remember that the Celts often liked to make their designs symmetrical – the same on either side.

▲ **3.** When you are happy with your design, glue the pieces in place.

# THE ROMANS IN BRITAIN

We know much more about the period when the Romans were in Britain than we do about earlier times. The Romans left written records of their activities, as well as many carved notices, called inscriptions, on monuments and buildings.

## GOVERNING A NEW LAND

As a province of the Roman Empire, Britain had a Roman governor who was responsible for running the country. He appointed local governors for towns and areas. The Roman army was always active to remind people of the Romans' strength and to tackle any uprisings that took place. Many Roman soldiers settled in Britain when they retired.

*Roman towns were built to a similar plan all over the empire, with straight streets, shops and houses, and a central market place called the forum. The Romans imported goods and food from all over the empire, helping Roman settlers to feel at home. Food plants such as carrots and peas were also introduced by the Romans.* ▼

*Tribes in the north of Scotland were never conquered by the Romans. In the second century AD the Emperor Hadrian had a wall built to stop them raiding further south. It was 120 kilometres (75 miles) long.*

## NEW WAYS OF LIVING

The Roman invaders brought many new ideas with them. Before the Romans came, there were no towns in Britain, only small villages. London, now the biggest city in Britain, was founded by the Romans.

## A WRITTEN LANGUAGE

The language of the Romans was Latin. They used it throughout their empire and every Roman soldier had to be able to read and write. Of course, Britons who lived and traded with the Romans had to learn Latin and many of them in the towns could read and write as well. For hundreds of years after the Romans left Britain, Latin was still used for official documents and in the Christian religion.

▲The Romans were skilled engineers. Their houses had plumbing and heating and they built roads and bridges throughout Britain. The Britons must have been astonished by the speed at which people and goods could be moved about the province.

This Roman mosaic floor from Fishbourne shows Cupid riding a dolphin, surrounded by sea beasts, sea horses and sea panthers.

## MANY BELIEFS

During the time that the Romans were in Britain, the new religion of Christianity, based on the teachings of Jesus Christ, began to spread to all parts of the empire.

The religion of the ancient Britons was closely linked to the natural world and the importance of the seasons and the fertility of the soil. Priests called druids led ceremonies and made predictions. The religion of the Romans featured many gods, some of whom also represented the rhythms of nature.

As long as local religions did not threaten their rule, the Romans let them continue. At first the Romans tried to stop Christianity because Christians claimed that their first duty was to God, not earthly rulers, but later even the Roman emperors became Christians.

9

# THE END OF AN EMPIRE

For nearly 400 years the Romans ruled a large part of the British Isles. Sometimes the Britons lived peacefully under Roman rule. But very often the Romans had to cope with uprisings by some of the British tribes or attacks from outside the borders of the empire.

A famous revolt happened only 16 years after the invasion. It was led by Boudica, queen of the Iceni tribe from East Anglia. Boudica's troops burnt down the town of Colchester and went on to attack and destroy London. The Roman governor, Suetonius, hurried back from Anglesey, where he was attacking other tribes, and crushed the British revolt.

*A later Roman historian described Boudica as having red hair and "a large golden necklace". It may have been like this neck-ring, called a torque, found in Norfolk.*

The problems that the Romans had in keeping order in Britain happened throughout the empire. As the empire grew, there were more people to control and more tribes outside the empire wanting to attack and steal from wealthy citizens. In AD 406 the Roman army finally left Britain to defend other parts of the empire. The end of the empire was very near and the Romans never returned.

*The Roman army was divided into legions and every legion had a standard called an "eagle". It was used as a rallying point during battles and was fiercely guarded.*

# MAKE A ROMAN STANDARD

▲ **1.** Draw an eagle shape like this on a piece of card and cut it out carefully. It should be about twice as wide as the paper plate.

**2.** Draw round the paper plate on to card to make a crescent shape and cut it out.

▲ **3.** Carefully cut the flat middle from the paper plate, making sure to cut the outer ring in only one place.

▲ **4.** Paint all the cut-out pieces and the pot-plant stake gold. Paint a piece of paper gold on both sides and cut out lots of leaf shapes. Stick them on to the ring from the paper plate to make a laurel wreath.

**You will need:** a garden cane at least 1 metre long ●cardboard ●a pencil ●a pot-plant stake ●a paper plate ●paper ●a piece of red or purple cloth ●scissors ●sticky tape or glue ●gold paint

▲ **5.** Hang the red or purple cloth from the pot-plant stake. You can fray the bottom edge and paint it to make a gold fringe if you like. Use sticky tape to fix all the pieces one under the other on the cane.

# A New Threat

While the Romans were in Britain, they defended their province from attacks by overseas tribes. But when the Roman army had gone, the British were at the mercy of invaders from northern Europe. Almost immediately, the people we describe as Anglo-Saxons began to attack the north-east coast of England.

## WHO WERE THE ANGLO-SAXONS?

The people that we call Anglo-Saxons actually came from several different tribes: the Jutes from what is now Denmark, the Angles from northern Germany, and the Saxons and Frisians from parts of Germany and the Netherlands. Their pirate ships had raided the coast of Britain for years, but when the Romans left they were able to push further into the country with greater numbers of people.

The parts of Europe where the Anglo-Saxons lived were difficult to farm. They were wooded and marshy, with some areas being flooded by the sea. There was not enough good land to feed everyone, so the Anglo-Saxons hoped to find better farming land in Britain.

North Sea

JUTES

ANGLES

SAXONS

FRISIANS

BRITONS

ANGLO-SAXON SETTLEMENT

5TH CENTURY

7TH CENTURY

▲ As the Anglo-Saxons gradually occupied more and more of Britain, they pushed some of the Celtic Britons further westward. But other Britons lived peacefully alongside the newcomers. It is from the Angles that we get the words "England" and "English".

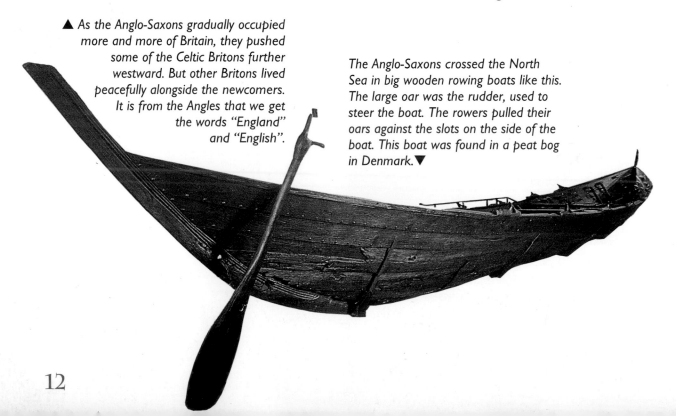

The Anglo-Saxons crossed the North Sea in big wooden rowing boats like this. The large oar was the rudder, used to steer the boat. The rowers pulled their oars against the slots on the side of the boat. This boat was found in a peat bog in Denmark.▼

# THE ANGLO-SAXON STORY OF THE INVASION

Over 400 years after the Anglo-Saxons began to arrive, King Alfred ordered that a book should be written to tell the history of the Anglo-Saxons in Britain. This book has survived and is called The Anglo-Saxon Chronicle. The book says that after the Romans left, a British king called Vortigern gave some Saxons land in south-east England in return for helping him to fight the Picts, a Scottish tribe that the Romans never conquered. Angles and Jutes, as well as Saxons, came to Britain, led by two brothers, Hengist and Horsa. When they had helped the king, the Chronicle says, they turned against him and took over the kingdom.

▲ This is a page from the Anglo-Saxon Chronicle. As the story was written down a long time after the events it describes, it is hard to tell whether it is true, but it is certainly possible that some Anglo-Saxons were invited to Britain.

# HOW ANGLO-SAXONS LIVED

The Anglo-Saxons did not invade Britain all at once but gradually moved down the rivers and settled further and further west and south. In some places Roman systems of government may have continued for up to 200 years after the Romans left. Meanwhile some Celtic British groups were returning to the way of life they followed before the Romans came. So for some time there was a great mixture of people and ways of life in Britain.

The Anglo-Saxon farmers grew peas, beans, barley and wheat as well as hay for their animals to eat in the winter. They kept cattle, sheep, pigs, geese and hens. They also seem to have had pet cats and dogs.

Many pieces of Anglo-Saxon pottery have been found. Most of these were for everyday use, but some pots were used as urns in which to bury the ashes of dead people.

There was no tea or coffee in England in Anglo-Saxon times. Poor people drank a kind of beer, while rich people had wine or mead, made from honey and water.

Most Anglo-Saxon clothes were made from wool. They raised the sheep, spun, dyed and wove the wool themselves. The weaving looms had stones with holes in them to weight down the threads. They were used leaning against the wall of a house.

Clothes were held together with brooches. Women wore strings of coloured glass or stone beads. Some women wore strange key-like metal objects from their waists. Archaeologists are not sure what these were for. What do you think?

# An Anglo-Saxon Village

Anglo-Saxon homes were usually built with a wooden framework. The walls were filled in with wooden planks or clay mixed with straw. Some of them seem to have had a space under the floor, perhaps for storage or to keep the floor dry.

A family home was quite small and probably had only one room. But the village also had a larger building, called a hall, where people could meet and eat together.

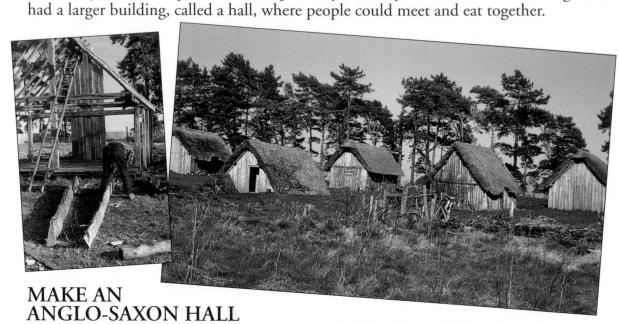

## MAKE AN ANGLO-SAXON HALL

▲ At West Stow in Suffolk, archaeologists have discovered traces of an Anglo-Saxon village. After finding post holes in the ground, they were able to work out where the village buildings were and make some good guesses about how they were built. Then they used this knowledge to rebuild the village using the same tools and methods that the Anglo-Saxons used.

**You will need:** thick cardboard
- newspaper • scissors • PVA glue
- sticky tape • a large plastic container
- paints

▲ **1.** Make a rectangular base about 35 cm long and 20 cm wide from a piece of strong cardboard. Then fold pieces of newspaper in halves and quarters and roll them up tightly. Use glue or sticky tape to make sure they don't unroll. Make two cuts at the end off each roll and glue or tape them evenly around the rectangle to make posts for your hall.

**2.** Trim the posts so that they are all the same level but shape the end ones as shown. Tape or glue more paper rolls across the posts as in the picture to make the framework for the roof and doors and windows.

▲ **3.** Tear some more newspapers into small pieces and soak them in water overnight in the plastic container.

**4.** Mash up the paper a bit more with your fingers. Then squeeze out as much water as possible and mix in some PVA glue. Add enough so that the paper can be modelled into different shapes.

**5.** Use the paper mixture to fill in the walls of the hall, just as the Anglo-Saxons used clay and straw. Remember to leave some spaces for windows and doors.

▲ **6.** When the paper mixture has dried, make a cardboard roof for your hall and put it carefully on top of the walls. Make sure it has a hole in the middle for smoke from the fire to come out.

▲ **7.** Paint your model and its base. You can add cardboard doors as well if you like.

Why not make lots of Anglo-Saxon buildings of different sizes and build a model village?

# RELIGIOUS LIFE

Christianity had come to Britain in Roman times, but the Anglo-Saxons brought their own religion. They believed that different gods controlled different parts of their lives and what would happen to them after they died.

Woden was the chief of all the gods. Frig, his wife, made crops grow. Tiu was the war god, and Thunor the god of thunder and the sky.

Our only clues to how the Anglo-Saxons worshipped their gods come from the writings of Christian missionaries who said that they killed animals in their religious ceremonies. But the missionaries were trying to stamp out the Anglo-Saxon religion, so it is hard to know if this is true.

*This Anglo-Saxon helmet and buckle are beautifully decorated. Often, Anglo-Saxon decorations contained images of the god Woden.*

*These objects were found in a grave at Sutton Hoo in Suffolk. An important man had been buried in a wooden boat that was 28 metres long. Many precious objects were buried with him. Although this was not a Christian burial, some objects with Bible names were found in the grave.* ▼

## AN ANGLO-SAXON BURIAL

Many of the pieces of Anglo-Saxon jewellery, goods and clothing that have been found were discovered in graves. In pagan (not Christian) burials, it seems that people were buried with some of their precious possessions, perhaps because it was thought that they would need them in the next life.

## THE RETURN OF CHRISTIANITY

By the time the Anglo-Saxons had been in Britain for about 200 years, Christianity was still practised in only a few western areas. Pope Gregory, the leader of the Christian religion in western Europe, sent a man called Augustine to England to convert the people to Christianity.

Christians believe that there is only one God and that he sent Jesus Christ to live on earth and show people how to act in this life and how they can live for ever with God after they die.

Augustine's first success was in converting Aethelbert, an Anglo-Saxon king living in Kent. The king allowed Augustine to use an old Roman church in Canterbury. Pope Gregory made Augustine Archbishop of Canterbury. This has been the title of the leader of the main Christian church in Britain ever since.

19

# MONASTERIES

Because the Anglo-Saxons did not invade Ireland, the people there were still Christians since Roman times. About 30 years before Augustine came to England, an Irish monk called Columba sailed to Iona, a small island off the western coast of Scotland, and built a monastery.

Monks are men who have decided to live together and make worshipping God the most important part of their lives. The place where they live is called a monastery. Women who do the same thing are called nuns. They live in a nunnery or convent.

Christianity spread across northern England and another famous monastery was built on the island of Lindisfarne, just off the coast of Northumbria.

▲ Lindisfarne's isolated position off the coast, later made it easy for raider's from the sea to attack.

Monasteries were important centres of learning for hundreds of years. The monks studied the Bible, the book that describes the life of Jesus Christ and the history of the people he lived among, and many other subjects. They wrote books by hand and often decorated them with beautiful coloured drawings.

◀ This is a page from the Lindisfarne Gospels. The Gospels are the part of the Bible that describes the life of Jesus. The book was copied out by hand and has many beautiful decorations. It is written in the Latin language on vellum, which is made from calf's skin.

# MAKE AN ILLUMINATED MANUSCRIPT

**You will need:** thick white or cream paper ● some strong, cold tea ● a sponge ● a pencil ● felt-tip pens ● a gold felt-tip pen

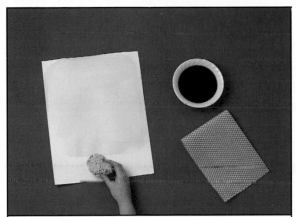

▲ **1.** Dip the sponge in the cold tea and dab it across the paper to make it look old. You could roughen or tear the edges a little bit too. Make the places where you think fingers would touch the page to turn it over a little darker still.

▲ **3.** Colour your design using felt-tip pens. To complete it, highlight some parts with the gold felt-tip pen.

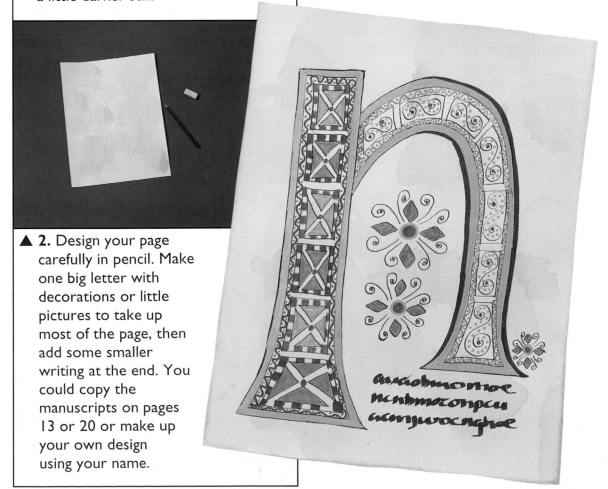

▲ **2.** Design your page carefully in pencil. Make one big letter with decorations or little pictures to take up most of the page, then add some smaller writing at the end. You could copy the manuscripts on pages 13 or 20 or make up your own design using your name.

# THE RULERS OF BRITAIN

When the Anglo-Saxons first came to Britain, they lived in small family groups. As they took control of more of England, they became organised into larger groups with a local chief or king. The names given to the areas under each king remain today in some of our county names. If Essex means "the kingdom of the East Saxons", what do you think Wessex and Sussex might mean?

*As well as the main kingdoms shown on the map, there were probably many independent kings ruling small areas.*

Each person had a different place and a different value in the kingdom. The Anglo-Saxons actually developed a system called "wergild" to set a value on people. This meant that each person was worth an amount of money.

The king was worth a lot of money, while a slave was worth very little. Everyone else came somewhere in between. If a person was killed, the killer had to pay the victim's family the amount he or she was worth.

As some of the kingdoms became more powerful, they tried to take over neighbouring areas. The first man to call himself "King of the English" was Offa, king of Mercia. His power and influence reached into the other kingdoms south of the River Humber.

▲*This great bank of earth with a ditch running beside it was built on the orders of King Offa. It is 238 kilometres long, stretching the length of Wales and separating it from Mercia. We don't know for certain why Offa's Dyke was built, but it shows that he was powerful.*

◀ *Offa had coins made with his name stamped on them.*

Offa ruled from 757 to 796, but by the time of his death, a new danger was threatening the peace of Britain. Once again, raiders from northern Europe were attacking. In 793 Vikings attacked the monastery at Lindisfarne and destroyed it.

The Vikings were excellent seamen and fierce fighters who came from Denmark, Norway and Sweden. For over 200 years they raided the coasts of Europe, but as traders they travelled even further   to Russia and central Asia. Some people think that they reached America as well, 600 years before Christopher Columbus.

Many of the Vikings who attacked Britain came from Denmark and were known as Danes, Northmen or Norsemen.

The Anglo-Saxons were very afraid of the Viking raiders. A common prayer was, "From the fury of the Northmen, good Lord deliver us."

# ALFRED AND LATER KINGS

At first the Vikings were mainly interested in raiding – taking what valuables they could find and disappearing again. But as time went on, the Vikings wanted more from Britain. Like the Anglo-Saxons before them, they did not have enough farming land at home to feed everyone and needed to find new lands. In 860 a large army of Vikings arrived from Denmark. The Anglo-Saxons called these Danes the "Great Army".

The Great Army attacked East Anglia and Northumbria and killed their kings. Then they moved into Mercia. Finally, only Wessex was not controlled by the new invaders.

## ALFRED "THE GREAT"

When a man called Alfred became King of Wessex, the Danes had already been attacking for some time. The leader of the Great Army, Guthrun, attacked Alfred at Chippenham during the Christmas celebrations, forcing the king to escape and hide at Athelney, in the marshes of Somerset. But from there Alfred organised his forces and defeated the Danes at Edington in 878.

▲ *After their defeat in 878, the Danes agreed to settle in the area shown in orange.*

## DANELAW

The Danes agreed to leave Wessex, part of Mercia and south-east England alone and to settle in Northumbria, East Anglia and the rest of Mercia. This area was known as Danelaw. Guthrun became a Christian.

◀ *After defeating the Danes, Alfred built fortified towns, called "burhs", where people could be safe if the Danes attacked again. This is where our word "borough" comes from. Like Roman towns hundreds of years before, Alfred's burhs had a rectangular shape and straight streets. This is a photograph of Wareham, Dorset, where the burh's street plan can still be seen.*

*This jewel was found in 1693, near Athelney. Words around the jewel say, "Aelfred mec heht gewyrcan" meaning "Alfred had me made". It shows what a wealthy and powerful man Alfred was.*

## THE IMPORTANCE OF LEARNING

Although he himself only learnt to read and write when he was grown up, Alfred was concerned about the Anglo-Saxon language and education.

He had several important Latin books translated into Anglo-Saxon, which is an early form of our modern English language. The Anglo-Saxon Chronicle was begun by him. Alfred's actions helped to create the feeling of a country with a history – an idea of "Englishness".

*While Alfred made his position safe in the south, more and more Vikings settled in northern England, trading with other parts of Europe. Wealthy towns grew up at places such as York and Nottingham.*

## ENGLAND AFTER ALFRED

It was Alfred's grandson, Athelstan, who, 50 years after Alfred fled to Athelney, marched his armies north and made the Viking and Welsh kings swear loyalty to him. For the first time, one man really was King of England, with most of Wales and Scotland also under his rule. But Athelstan and the kings who came after him still had battles to fight.

# THE LAST CONQUEROR

Nearly 40 years after Athelstan's death, the Vikings once again began to attack Britain. King Ethelred agreed to pay money to the Danes if they would go home! This was called "Danegeld" and for a while it worked. But in 1013 King Swein of Denmark attacked and seized the throne, beginning nearly 30 years of Danish rule.

**Saxons**
924 – 39 Athelstan
939 – 46 Edmund
946 – 55 Edred
955 – 59 Edwy
959 – 75 Edgar
975 – 78 Edward (the Martyr)
978 – 1013 Ethelred (the Unready)

**Danes**
1013 – 14 Swein
1014 – 35 Cnut
1035 – 40 Harold I
1040 – 42 Harthacnut

**Saxons**
1042 – 66 Edward the Confessor
1066 Harold II

**Normans**
William I (the Conqueror)

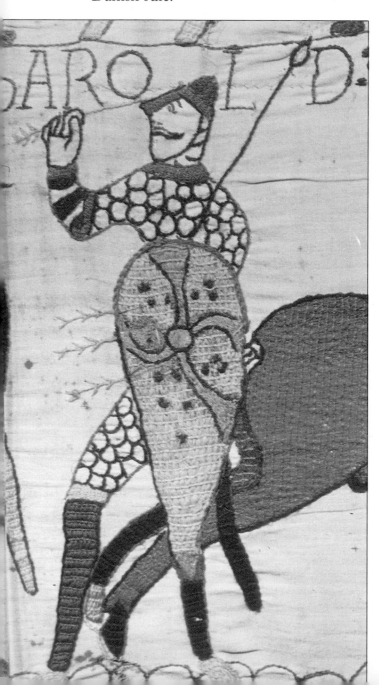

Swein's son, Cnut, married Emma, the widow of Ethelred. She was a Norman princess from Normandy in northern France. When Edward the Confessor died without any children in 1066, he promised the throne to William, the Duke of Normandy, but the English decided to crown Harold, the Earl of Wessex instead.

As soon as Harold was crowned, he faced trouble. The Norwegians invaded northern England in September and Harold marched north to defeat them. In the meantime, William landed in Sussex to claim the throne. Harold's exhausted army met the Normans at Hastings and Harold was killed.

*The Bayeux tapestry, which shows the story of William's claim to the English throne, was embroidered by Anglo-Saxon women in France. This part shows the death of King Harold.*

William's coronation on Christmas Day, 1066, marked the end of Anglo-Saxon rule in England but William's position was not yet secure. Accepting the crown of the Anglo-Saxon kings was one of his first acts to take control of the kingdom.

◀ *This engraving shows William being crowned King of England at Westminster Abbey.*

## MAKE WILLIAM'S CROWN

**You will need:** thin card • a ruler • a pencil • scissors • gold paint • paper clips

▲ **1.** Draw a shape on to thin card and cut it out carefully. Make it about 12 cm high.

▲ **2.** Take a piece of card about 50 cm long and draw a line right along it 6 cm from the edge. Make a mark at 5 cm along the line, at 15 cm, 25 cm, 35 cm and 45 cm.

▲ **3.** At each mark draw round your card shape above the line.

**4.** Carefully cut out the crown and paint it gold. Fix the two ends together with paper clips or sticky tape, overlapping the ends to give a good fit.

# THE INVADERS LEGACY

All the invaders of Britain from the Romans to the Normans have left traces of their lives that we can still see today.

## PLACE NAMES

The names of our towns and villages are clues to who lived there in the past. The Romans, the Anglo-Saxons and the Vikings used their own languages to name places. Sometimes the spelling of these has changed over the years. Look at the lists below. Then find a map of your area and see if you can tell which people named the towns and villages nearby. Books about place names in your local library will give you even more information about their meaning.

### Roman place names

| | | |
|---|---|---|
| camp | = | plain |
| caster | = | fort |
| eccles | = | church |
| port | = | harbour |
| wic | = | town |

### Anglo-Saxon place names

| | | |
|---|---|---|
| burg, borough | = | fortified place |
| den, dene | = | valley |
| ea, ey | = | river |
| feld, field | = | field |
| ford | = | shallow river crossing |
| ham | = | settlement home |
| head | = | hill |
| holt | = | dense wood |
| ing | = | people |
| lea, leigh, ley | = | clearing |
| mere | = | lake |
| sted, stead | = | place |
| stoke, stow | = | meeting place |
| ton, tun | = | farm or village |
| wald | = | wood |
| wic, wick, wich | = | farm |
| worth | = | hedged land |

### Viking place names

| | | |
|---|---|---|
| by | = | village |
| thorpe | = | small village |

## THE ENGLISH LANGUAGE

Some of our names for the days of the week also come from Britain's invaders. Sunday and Monday are named after the sun and moon, while Saturday takes its name from the Roman god, Saturn. Look at pages 18 and 19 and see if you can work out where the names of the other days of the week come from.

Many other common English words come from Anglo-Saxon. Below are a few of them:

cald, penig, cyssan, grund, abbod, lang, Englisc, gewyrcan

Can you guess what they mean? Look at the box on the left if you get stuck.

**Answers** The Anglo-Saxon words mean: cold, penny, kiss, ground, abbot, long, English. Look on page 24 for a clue to "gewyrcan" and remember that in order to make something, you have to "work."

# DID YOU KNOW?

Until about 9,000 years ago, Britain was joined to the rest of Europe. People could simply walk across. But gradually the sea rose and Britain became an island. The only way to reach it was by boat.

When the Emperor Claudius came to Colchester to accept the surrender of some British leaders, he even brought a few elephants along to impress the Britons with his power! Of course, they had never seen such creatures before.

One way of writing Anglo-Saxon words was to use "runes". You can see which letters the runes stood for below. The Anglo-Saxons seem to have thought that the runes themselves were magic. They wrote the alphabet on rings as a charm against illness and danger.

In a way the Vikings really did succeed in conquering Britain. The Normans who invaded in 1066 were descended from "Norsemen" who had settled in northern France 200 years earlier.

The legend of King Arthur and his knights of the round table is set in the period when Anglo-Saxon raiders were attacking British tribes. All the old writings about Arthur date from hundreds of years later, so it is very hard to tell whether a British king called Arthur really existed.

ᚠ ᚢ ᚦ ᚩ ᚱ ᚳ ᚷ ᚹ ᚻ ᚾ ᛁ ᛄ ᚻ ᛈ

f u th o r k g w h n i j h p

ᛉ ᛋ ᛏ ᛒ ᛖ ᛗ ᛚ ᛝ ᛞ ᛟ ᚪ ᚫ ᚣ ᛠ

x s t b e m l ng d oe a ae y ea

# GLOSSARY

**archaeologist** – someone who studies objects from past times, often those that are buried in the ground.

**burh** – a fortified town that King Alfred ordered to be built.

**Danegeld** – money paid by Anglo-Saxon kings to Danish leaders to try to stop them from invading Britain.

**daub** – mud or clay used to fill the gaps in walls made of wattle.

**earthwork** – a structure made mainly of earth and stones, often as a place of safety.

**empire** – a large area of land, often made up of different countries, ruled over by one person, an emperor or empress.

**forum** – the main square and market place of a Roman town.

**inscription** – written words, especially those on a building, gravestone or coin.

**invader** – a person who moves into a new area without the permission of people already living there.

**javelin** – a kind of spear that could be thrown at the enemy.

**legion** – a body of between 3,000 and 6,000 men in the Roman army.

**missionary** – a person who tries to convert others to a particular religious faith.

**monastery** – a place where monks live – Christians who live together to devote their lives to God.

**monument** – a building or statue put up to remind people of a person or event.

**rudder** – a piece of wood under a boat that can be turned to change the boat's direction.

**settler** – a person who makes his or her home in a new place.

**torque** – a necklace of twisted metal made by the ancient Britons.

**vellum** – calf's skin made smooth so that it could be written on.

**wattle** – twigs woven together to make walls.

**wergild** – an Anglo-Saxon system of setting a value of money on each person. If the person was killed, the killer could pay that money to the family of the victim and avoid further punishment.

# RESOURCES

## PLACES TO VISIT

Many museums have objects from Celtic, Roman, Anglo-Saxon, Viking or Norman times. Local museums often display historical objects that have been found in the area. Ask your local tourist information centre for advice on where to visit.

### British Museum

Great Russell Street
London
WC1B 3DG
The British Museum has most of the important objects found in Britain, including treasures from the Sutton Hoo burial.

### Jorvik Viking Centre

Coppergate
York
YO1 9WT
Travel by 'time car' through the sights, smells and sounds of an historical reconstruction showing part of Viking York.

### Sutton Hoo

Tranmer House
Sutton Hoo
Woodbridge
IP12 3DJ
Visit the burial ground of the Anglo-Saxon kings of East Anglia and the excellent Exhibition Hall.

### West Stow Anglo-Saxon Village

Icklingham Road
West Stow
Bury St Edmunds
IP28 6HG
Walk around this reconstructed Anglo-Saxon village and look at original Anglo-Saxon objects that were found on the site.

### Norman castles

The Normans built castles to keep control of the English people. You can still visit many of them today.

## USEFUL WEBSITES

www.bbc.co.uk/schools/anglosaxons
Informative BBC website about the Anglo-Saxons, with a timeline and activities.

www.bbc.co.uk/schools/romans
This BBC site includes information, activities and games about the Romans.

www.bbc.co.uk/schools/vikings
Another good BBC site, this time about the Vikings.

www.bbc.co.uk/scotland/education/sysm/romans/index_choice.shtml
Take an on-line tour around a Roman fort or Caledonian village to learn about the Romans in Scotland.

www.thebritishmuseum.ac.uk/explore/families_and_children/online_tours.aspx
Click on 'Anglo-Saxons' for an on-line tour of some of the best objects in the British Museum's collection. Also click on 'Sutton Hoo' for information about nine objects relating to this Anglo-Saxon burial.

**Note to parents and teachers:** Every effort has been made by the Publishers to ensure that these websites are suitable for children, that they are of the highest educational value, and that they contain no inappropriate or offensive material. However, because of the nature of the Internet, it is impossible to guarantee that the contents of these sites will not be altered. We strongly advise that Internet access is supervised by a responsible adult.

# INDEX

## Additional Photographs:

Ancient Art & Architecture Collection 9, 10, 18, 20, 22, 26; British Library 13; ET Archive 6, 18, 24; Michael Halford 18, 19; Mansell Collection 27; Zefa 5, 8